Great Testing Tools for Great Testers:

A Guide to Recent & Obscure Testing Tools

By Mark Garzone

Copyright © 2016

Disclaimer

To Konrad Zuse, the inventor of the first programmable computer.

Preface

Why another book on software testing tools? This book was motivated by the lack of coverage of newer testing tools which have recently appeared on the testing market and also to cover less discussed tools in other testing books. This book presents tools which add power to a tester's arsenal of tools.

Table of Contents

Chapter 1: BDD Testing Tools

What is behaviour driven development? It is an extension of test driven development in which units tests are defined around feature behaviours based on examples. The unit tests are defined in an English like language format called Gherkin. Automation test tools such as SpecFlow and Cucumber convert these feature behaviours descriptions into skeleton unit tests that need to be later filled in by automation testers. The main advantage of BDD is that the business analysts can write features in structured English so that programmers and testers can understand it, and implement the code and automated tests.

The most common format for the examples is Given-When-Then which is the format you'll see mostly used by the BDD community. When you have a complex business rule with several variable inputs or outputs you might end up creating several scenarios that only differ by their values. Below is the format of a feature:

"Feature" describes the behavior feature.
"Scenario" describes a scenario of the feature (a business rule).
"Given" describes the initial context for the action.
"When" describes an event that happens due to an action that the actor in the system or stakeholder performs.
"Then" describes the action's expected outcome.

Here's an example of a feature stored in a .feature file:

Example:
Feature: Refund item
Scenario: Refunded clothing items should be returned to stock
Given a customer previously bought 1 blue shirt from me
And I currently have 3 blue shirts left in stock.
When he returns the blue shirt for a refund
Then I should have 4 blue shirts in stock

Often other scenarios are written as examples of values in a table for parameterized variables in brackets <>. See below:

Example:
Given there are <start> cucumbers
When I eat <eat> cucumbers
Then I should have <left> cucumbers
Examples:

| start | eat | left|

| 12 | 5 | 7 |

| 20 | 5 | 15|

See figure 1 for a Cucumber .feature file.

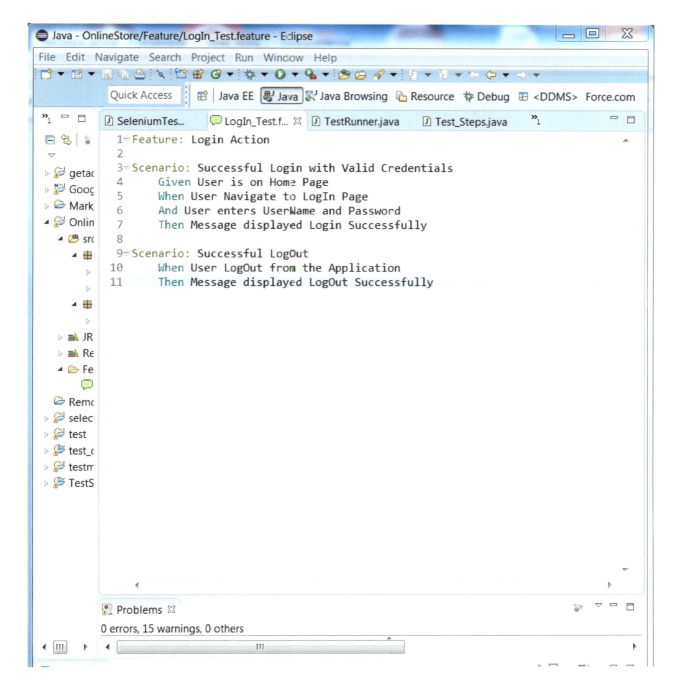

Figure 1

This feature example can feed to an automation tool (such as Behat, Cucumber or SpecFlow) that will transform it into the automated specification. Developers can then use this automated specification to drive the application development.

As a matter of fact, the language we used in the example of the previous section is Gherkin. Gherkin is a keyword-based, line-oriented language. This means that, except when you need to break sentences down into lines and use special reserved keywords, you are free to use actual ubiquitous language to write down behavior examples. This simpler format also makes it easy to support Gherkin in different programming languages. At the time of writing there are Gherkin automation tools which convert the features files into automation skeleton files written in languages such as Ruby, Python, PHP, .Net, JS, Java and its derivatives. See figure 2 for the automated Cucumber steps file by Gherkin.

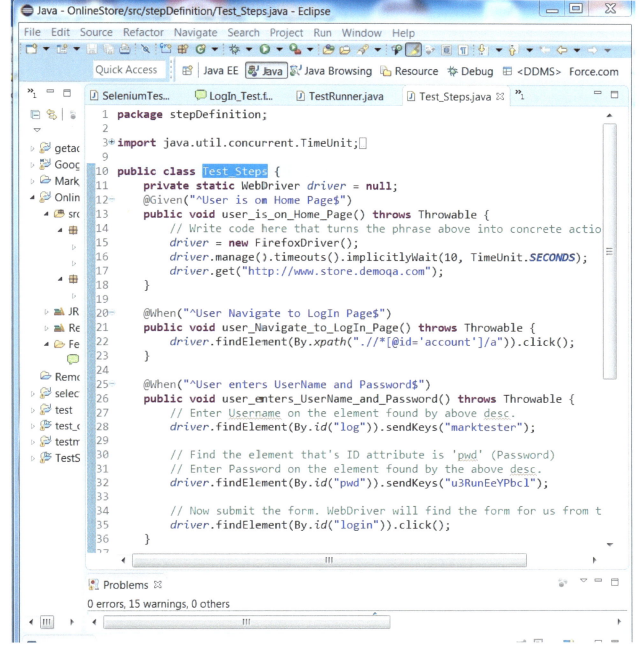

Figure 2

What's the best BDD framework? It depends on your language preference. Cucumber covers the most common programming languages. Here is a list of some of BDD frameworks by language.

- Ruby: Cucumber, Spinach

- Java: JBehave, JDave, Cucumber

- C#: NBehave, SpecFlow, Cucumber

- Python: Freshen, Lettuce

- PHP: Behat, Codeception, PhpUnit + Selenium

- JavaScript: Cucumber-JS, Yadda, Jasmine-species

- Flex: Cucumber

Squish

Squish is a BDD tool that uses Gherkin feature files without modification. The Squish IDE allows steps to be recorded for the BDD features. Test steps can also be implemented in any of Squish's scripting languages of Python, JavaScript, Ruby, Perl and TCL. Squish also allows BDD test cases and pure script test cases to be in the same single test suite. See figure 3 for the feature file and figure 4 for automated steps file by Gherkin in Squish.

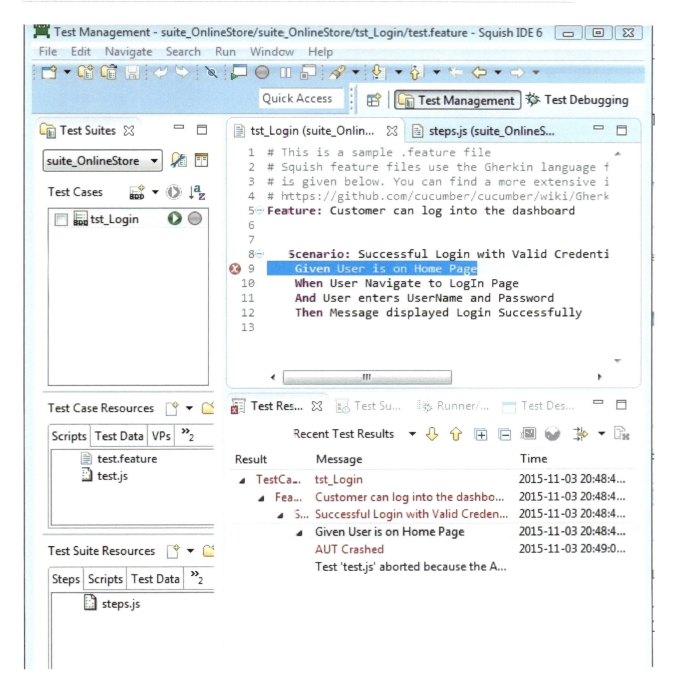

Figure 3

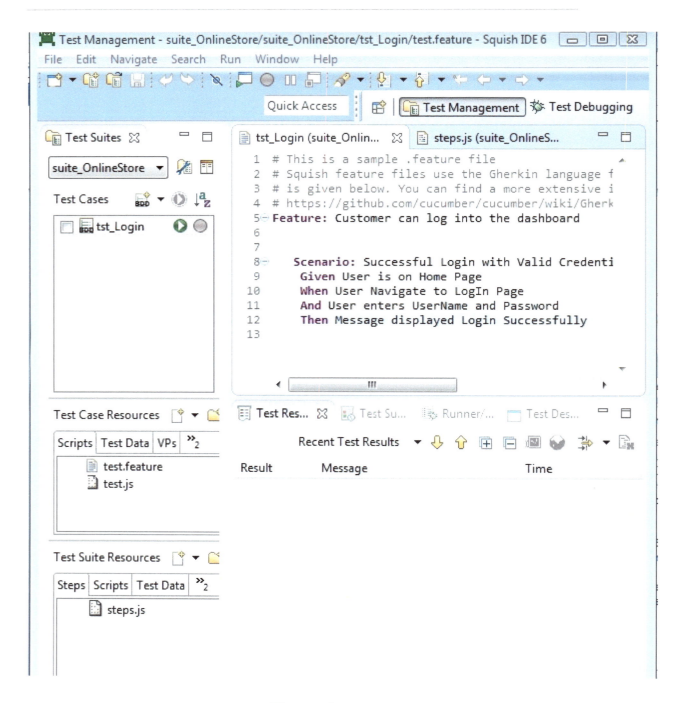

Figure 4

Chapter 2: Web Testing Tools

Web testing tools may be classified based on different prerequisites that a user may require to test web applications mainly scripting requirements, and GUI functionalities. Below is a list of testing tools for functionality testing, automated testing, cross-browser testing, accessibility testing, and usability testing. Security testing tools and performance testing tools are covered in other chapters.

Telerik

Test Studio by Telerik is a powerful testing tool that runs on windows for testing web apps, desktop apps and mobile apps. It's used for functional testing, automation testing, performance testing and mobile app testing. It has its own testing framework. See figure 5.

Some of the features include:

- Scriptless test recording playback.
- Running cross-browser automated tests in all popular browsers.
- Support for HTML, AJAX, Silverlight, .NET app testing.
- Integration with Visual Studio's Team Foundation Server.
- Unit testing integration with Nunit, MbUnit and XUnit.
- Build center integration with CruiseControl, MS Build Server, and TeamCity.
- Bug tracking tools integration.
- Fiddler web debugger integration.
- Test management tool integration with HP Quality Center.

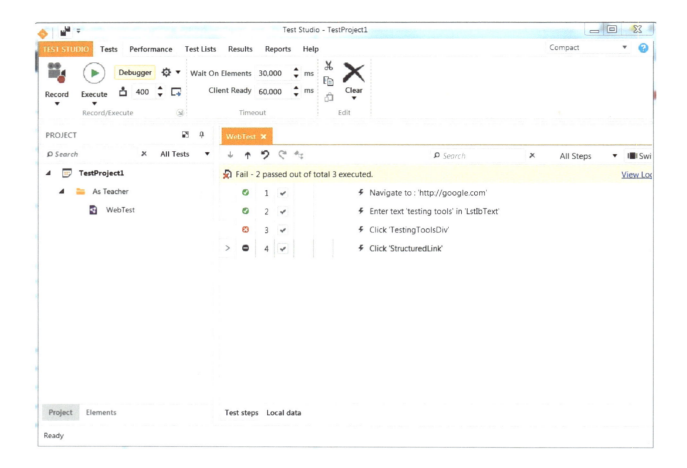

Figure 5

iMacros

iMacros is testing scripting tool for testing web apps. The free extension for Firefox, Chrome and Internet Explorer allows test scripts to be recorded and played back.

Along with the freeware version, iMacros has commercial editions that can automate Adobe Flash, Adobe Flex, Silverlight, and Java applets by using direct screen and image recognition technology. The freeware version of iMacros contains no control flow statements. The commercial version has conditional code for scripting. See figure 6.

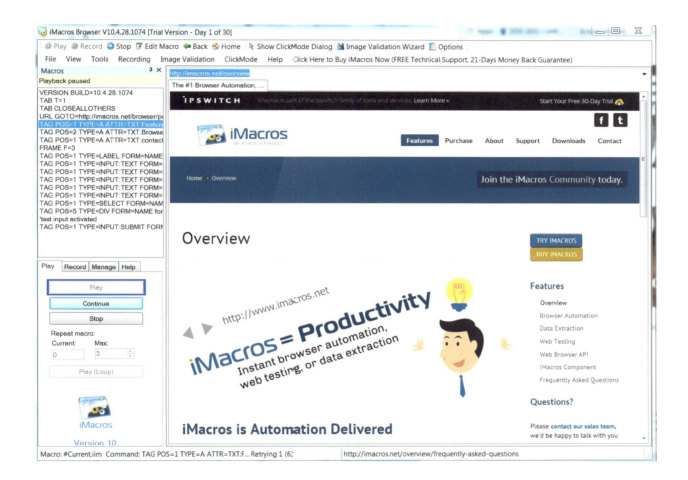

Figure 6

Powerfuzzer

Powerfuzzer is a highly automated and fully customizable web fuzzer which is based on other open source fuzzers. Fuzzers work by inputting massive amounts of random data, called fuzz, to the system in an attempt to make it crash. The powerfuzzer fuzzes the HTTP protocol. See figure 7.

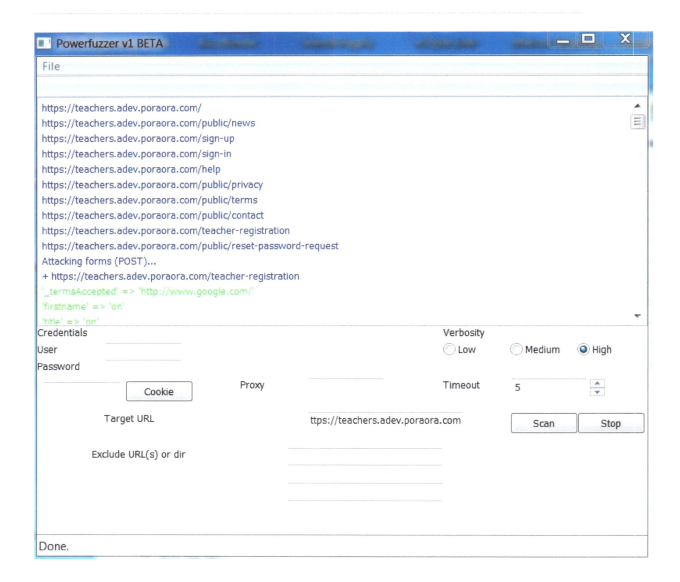

Figure 7

Robot Framework

Robot Framework is an open source test automation framework for acceptance testing and acceptance test-driven development (ATDD). Test cases are written using keyword testing methodology written in a tabular format. These tables can be written in plain text, HTML, tab-separated values (TSV), or reStructuredText (reST) formats files. Users can create new higher-level keywords from existing ones using the same syntax that is used for creating test cases. Robot framework is implemented in Python. See figure 8 for the command line run and figure 9 for a report example.

Also the Robot framework is integrated with Selenium using the library called Selenium2Libray. It contains keywords that trigger selenium actions. Examples include Open Browser, Focus Input Text, Input Password Click Button, Click Image, and Close Browser. Variables are used in most places in the test data. Most commonly, they are used in arguments for keywords in test case tables and keyword tables. An example variable is ${VALID USER}

Here is a valid login test case file:

```
*** Settings ***

Documentation  A test suite with a single test for valid login. This
test has a workflow that is created using keywords from the resource
file.
Resource        common_resource.txt


*** Test Cases ***

Valid Login
    Open Browser To Login Page
    Input Username     demo
    Input Password     mode
    Submit Credentials
    Welcome Page Should Be Open
    [Teardown]  Close Browser
```

Invalid Login test case example:

```
*** Settings ***
```

Documentation   A test suite containing tests related to invalid
login. These tests are data-driven by their nature. They use a
single keyword, specified with Test Template setting, that is called
with different arguments to cover different scenarios.
Suite Setup   Open Browser To Login Page
Test Setup   Go To Login Page
Test Template   Login With Invalid Credentials Should Fail
Suite Teardown   Close Browser
Resource   common_resource.txt

*** Test Cases ***   User Name   Password

Invalid Username   invalid ${VALID PASSWD}
Invalid Password ${VALID USER}   invalid
Invalid Username And Password   invalid   whatever
Empty Username ${EMPTY} ${VALID PASSWD}
Empty Password ${VALID USER} ${EMPTY}
Empty Username And Password ${EMPTY} ${EMPTY}

*** Keywords ***

Login With Invalid Credentials Should Fail
    [Arguments] ${username} ${password}
    Input Username ${username}
    Input Password ${password}
    Submit Credentials
    Login Should Have Failed

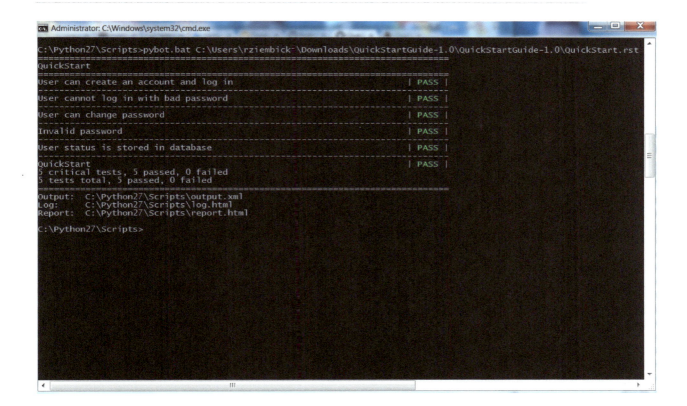

Figure 8

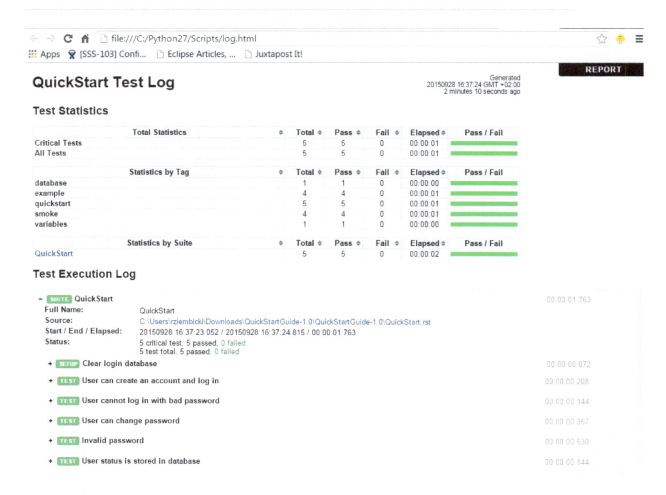

Figure 9

SPOF-O-MATIC

The tool SPOF-O-MATC is a Chrome extension which detects third-party single points of failure as you browse and allows you to simulate 3rd party resources being unavailable.

After installing it, to enable content blocking, click the greyed-out black hole icon in the toolbar. As you browse the icon in the toolbar will display a warning icon if you are on a site that is likely to have problems loading third-party content. If you click on the icon it will display the list of suspect resources as well as how much of the page content they block (resources closer to the top of the page will have more of a user impact). See figure 10.

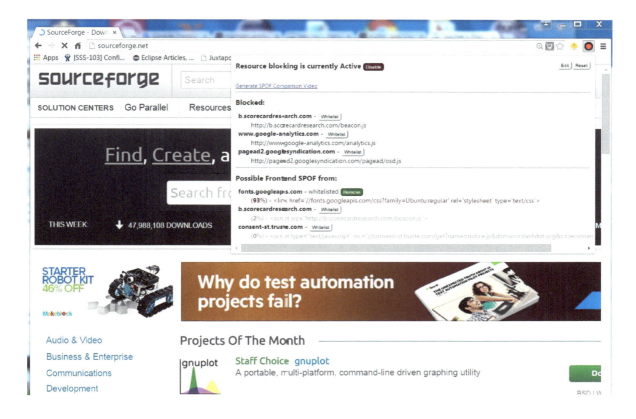

Figure 10

Firefox FireShot add-on

There are many screenshot apps out there such as Cropper, PicPick, and Skitch. FireShot is a FF plugin that takes full web page screenshots. See figure 11. It has the following nice features:

- Saved as Image or PDF
- Sent to clipboard
- Printed

- Annotated

- Uploaded

- E-Mailed

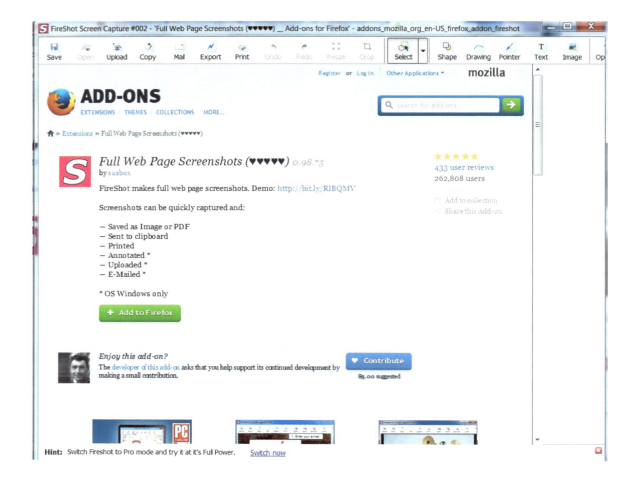

Figure 11

Firesizer

Firesizer is a great tool that allows you to resize the window to specific dimensions at the bottom of the browser right corner. See figure 12.

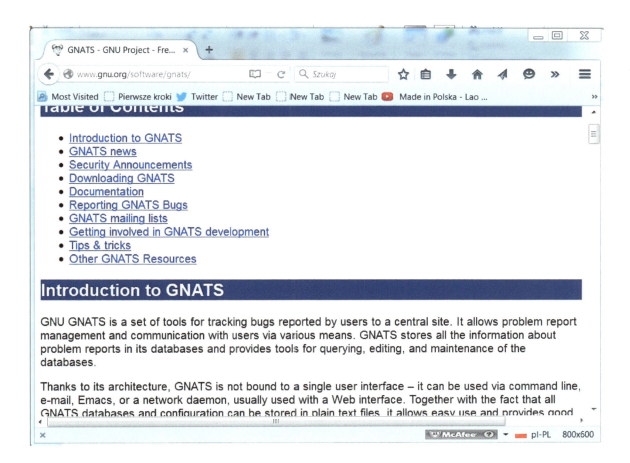

Figure 12

Firefox MeasureIt

This is nifty tool allows you to draw a ruler across any web page to check the width, height, or alignment of page elements in pixels. It is useful when you want to specify precisely some details of a GUI element in a bug report. See figure 13.

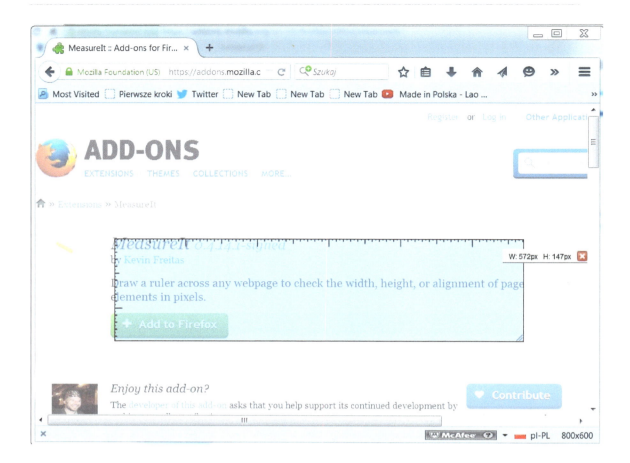

Figure 13

Jameleon

Jameleon is a data driven automated testing framework based on keywords or tags that represent different screens of an application. All of the logic required to automate each particular screen can be defined in Java and XML mapped to these keywords. The keywords can then be organized with different data sets to form test scripts without requiring an in-depth knowledge of how the application functions. The test scripts are then used to automate testing with data read from properties files, CSV files, and DB rows. Several plugins such as Selenum, Junit, and HTTPUnit are designed to interface with different apps under test. See figure 14 and 15.

Test cases are written as XML scripts using tags which can be generic ones or customized java implemented ones. Here is an example of a test case below.

```
<testcase xmlns="jelly:jameleon">
   <ju-session>
       <ju-assert-equals
            functionId="Compare two equaling values"
            expected="value 1"
            actual="value 1"/>
   </ju-session>
</testcase>
```

Here is another test case which reads values from a CSV file whose first header row is firstName_c

```
<testcase xmlns="jelly:jameleon" useCSV="true">
    <junit-session>
        <csr-customer-profile
 functionId="Change the customer's first name to
${firstName_c}"
                customerFirstName="${firstName_c}"/>
    </junit-session>

</testcase>
```

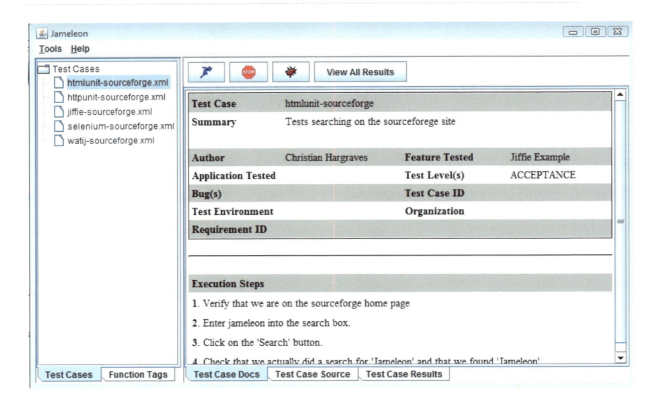

Figure 14

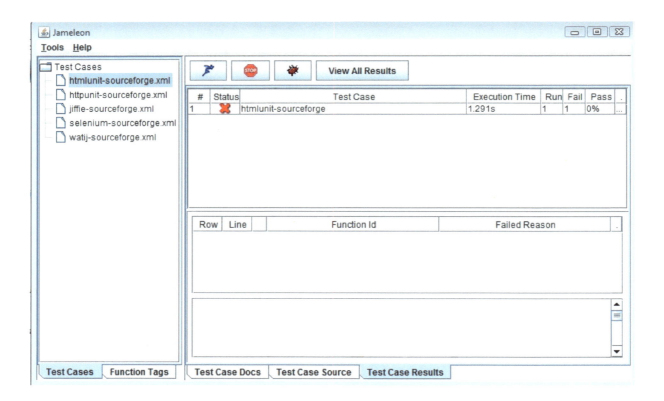

Figure 15

Postman

Postman is a free Chrome extension app testing tool for testing HTTP requests such as JSON requests. See figure 16. Post man has built-in authentication helpers. It comes with a testing framework that allows one to customize test scripts using JavaScript. Example snippets can be easily pulled into the tool IDE to allow for quick scripting. See figure 17. Tests are stored in collection which run every request and gives you an aggregate summary of what happened. It stores all your test runs so you can compare them and see what has changed. For a small extra monthly subscription the tests can be stored in the cloud and can be managed by a team of testers.

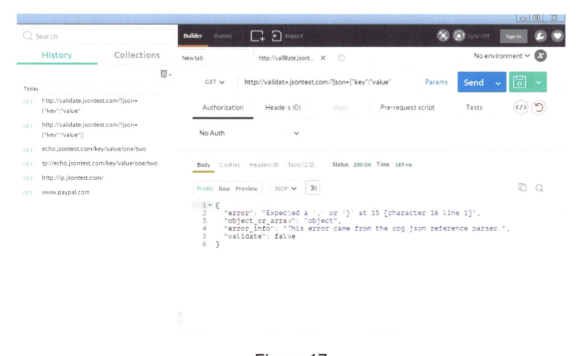

Figure 17

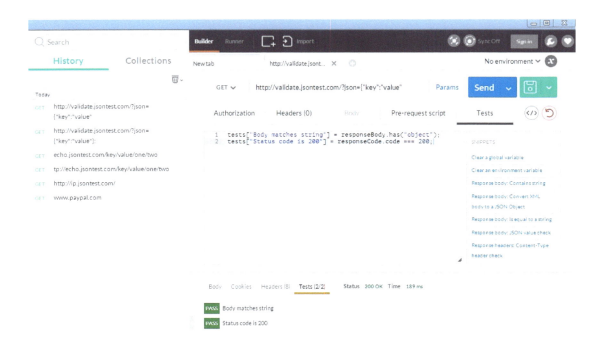

Figure 18

TestingBot

Testingbot runs cross browser tests in over 500 real browser combinations including Internet Explorer 6, 7, 8, 9, 10, 11 and Microsoft Edge. TestingBot offers Selenium testing for RC and WebDriver. Testingbot has examples to easily run your tests on a grid, available in any popular language and testing framework. Also tests can to run mobile tests on iPhone/iPad (iOS 8) and Android with Appium. See figure 19 and 20.

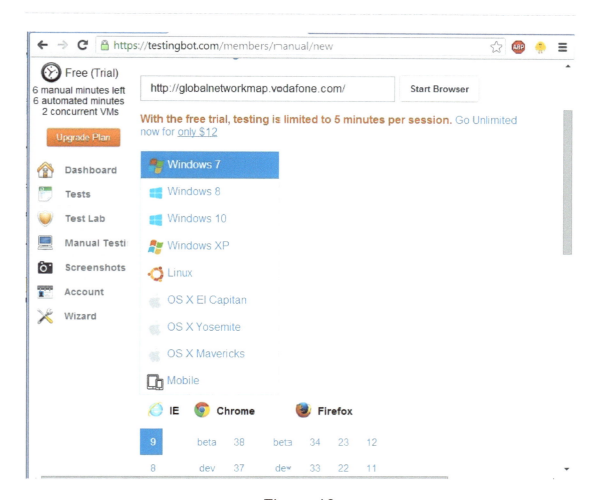

Figure 19

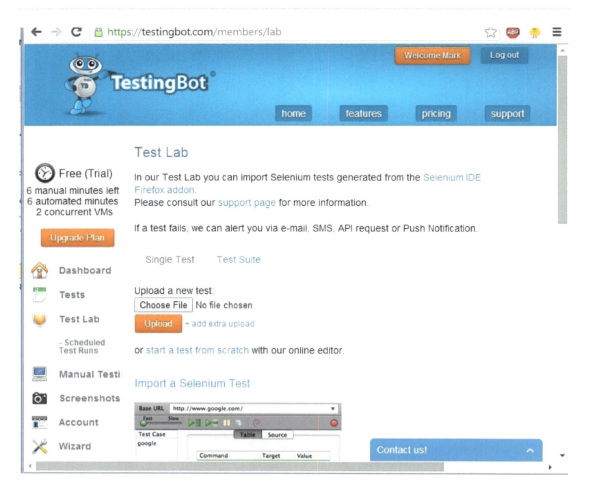

Figure 20

WebInject

WebInject is a free tool written in Perl for automated testing of web apps and web services. It can be used to test individual system components that have HTTP interfaces and can be used as a test harness to create an automated test suite. WebInject can run on any platform that a Perl interpreter can be installed. Test cases are written in XML files. These XML files are passed to the WebInject engine for execution against the application/service under test. Test result reports are generated in HTML and in XML. These detailed results include pass/fail status, errors, response times, etc. Results are also displayed in a window on the User Interface if you are running the WebInject GUI. The results are sent to the STDOUT channel if you are running the WebInject Engine as a standalone (console) application. See figure 21 and 22.

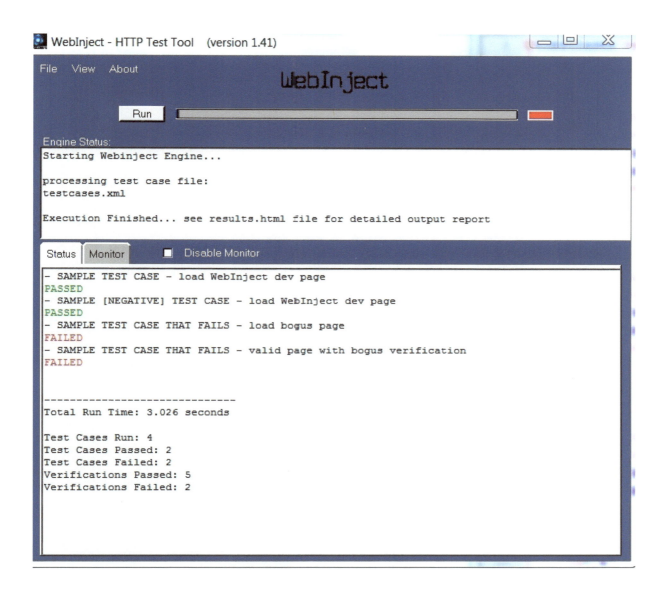

Figure 21

```
 1  ⊟<testcases repeat="1">
 2
 3   <case
 4       id="1"
 5       description1="SAMPLE TEST CASE - load WebInject dev page"
 6       description2="verify string 'Corey Goldberg' exists in response"
 7       method="get"
 8       url="http://www.webinject.org/dev.html"
 9       verifypositive="Corey Goldberg"
10   />
11
12   <case
13       id="2"
14       description1="SAMPLE [NEGATIVE] TEST CASE - load WebInject dev page"
15       description2="verify string 'bogus string' does not exist in response"
16       method="get"
17       url="http://www.webinject.org/dev.html"
18       verifynegative="bogus string"
19   />
20
21   <case
22       id="3"
23       description1="SAMPLE TEST CASE THAT FAILS - load bogus page"
24       description2="case should fail with an HTTP 404 (not found) error"
25       method="get"
26       url="http://www.webinject.org/bogus.html"
27   />
28
29   <case
30       id="4"
31       description1="SAMPLE TEST CASE THAT FAILS - valid page with bogus verification'
32       description2="case should fail"
33       method="get"
34       url="http://www.webinject.org/dev.html"
35       verifypositive="I am a bogus string"
36   />
37
```

Figure 22

Sahi

Sahi is a free open source tool for automation of web application testing. Sahi is especially suited for cross-browser/multi-browser testing of complex web apps with AJAX and dynamic content and JavaScript. See figure 22, 23, and 24.

Key Features

- Has a script recorder and object spy which works on Internet Explorer, Firefox, Chrome, Safari, Opera (and any modern browser).

- Playback on any desktop browser and on mobile browsers.

- Very simple and robust object identification mechanism which works across browsers. Sahi does not use XPaths or css selectors. It uses its own wrappers around the JavaScript DOM which are simple to use and easy to maintain. Sahi works even when elements do not have ids. Sahi uses relational APIs like _in, _near, _under, _leftOf, _rightOf etc. to uniquely identify elements. Sahi traverses across frames and iframes. Sahi automatically waits for page loads and AJAX activity. There is no need to add wait statements in 95% cases. This reduces the code base size by 50% compared to other tools. Sahi does not need require a browser to be in focus. Sahi can simultaneously playback multiple scripts reducing playback time. Sahi automatically creates rich reports without adding any extra code. This keeps the script simple. Sahi supports HTML5 custom tags and Shadow DOM.

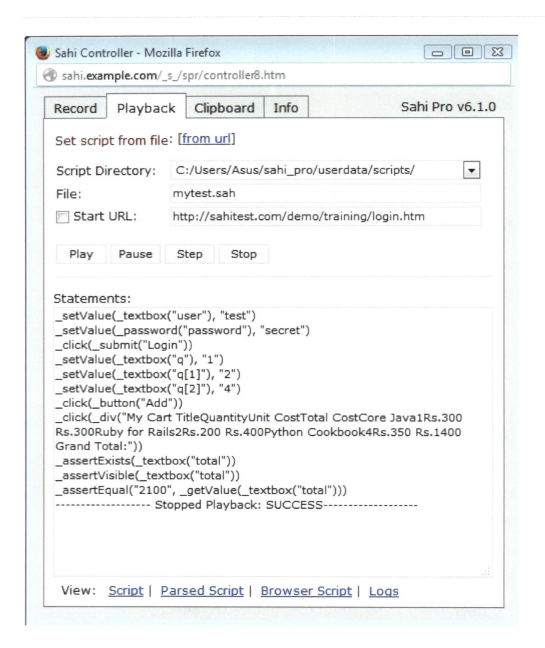

Figure 22

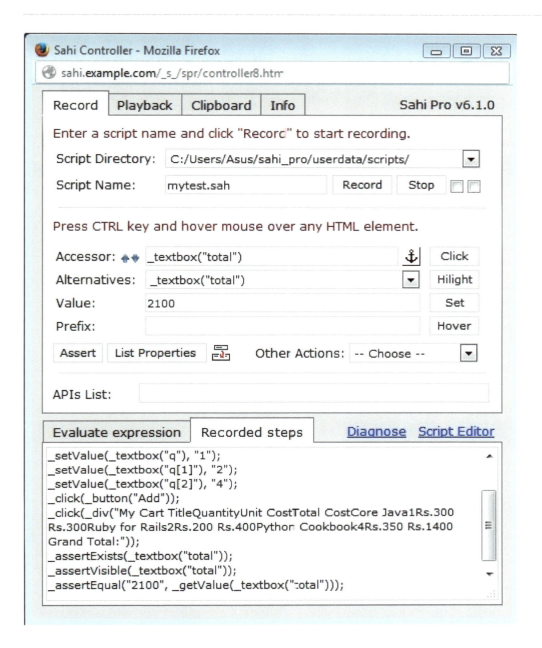

Figure 23

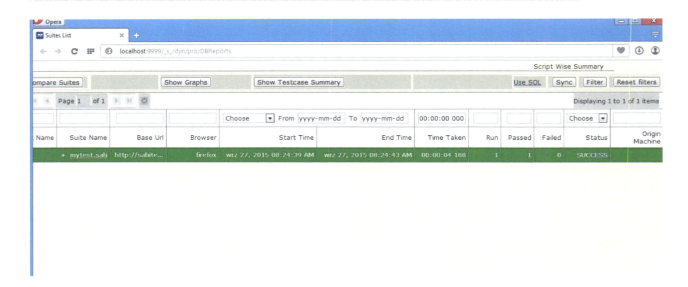

Figure 24

Check My Links

Check My Links is a link checker that crawls through a web page and looks for broken links. 'Check My Links' is a Chrome extension developed primarily for web designers, developers and testers. It color codes all the working links in green and all the invalid broken links in red. See figure 25.

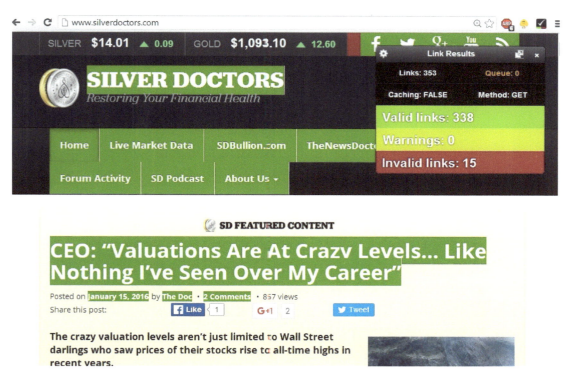

Figure 25

Dead Link Checker

Dead Link Checker is an online website which finds broken links on a website so that they can be fixed, and restore the site's rankings and attracting more web traffic. Link checking can a scheduled to run with the auto-checker service for your specified frequency and depth of scan. After completion of the scheduled scan a report is emailed with details of any dead links found. See figure 26 .

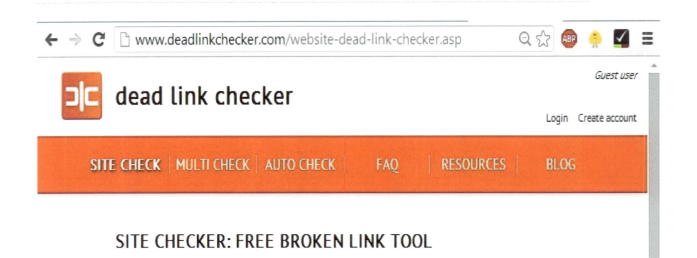

SITE CHECKER: FREE BROKEN LINK TOOL

http://www.paypal.com

○ Check whole website   ○ Check single webpage   pause

http://www.paypal.com
51% scanned - **903/1743** URLs checked, **890** OK, **13 failed**
Checking file: https://t.paypal.com/ts?
nojs=1&pgrp=main%3Amktg%3A%3Asignup%3Aaccountselect&page=main%3Amktg%3A%3Asignup%3Aac
selection.dust&pgst=Unknown&lgin=out&vers=&calc=72195c9d6701c&rsta=es_NI&pgtf=&s=ci&ccpg=ni&

Status	URL	Source link
403 Forbidden	https://www.paypalobjects.com/	link/href
-1 Not found: The	https://developer.paypal.com/	PayPal Developers
-1 Not found: A co	https://feedback-form.truste.com/watchdog/request	TRUSTe Watchdog Di
-1 Not found: The	https://myprofile.paypalcorp.com/MyProfile/	Find new ways to gro
-1 Not found: The	https://developer.paypal.com/webapps/developer/docs/classic/pr	Adaptive Payments
-1 Not found: The	https://developer.paypal.com/docs/classic/mobile/gs_MPL/	Android Mobile Paym
-1 Not found: The	https://developer.paypal.com	Find out more at Payl
-1 Not found: The	https://developer.paypal.com/webapps/developer/docs/classic/pr	MassPay API
-1 Not found: The	https://developer.paypal.com/docs/classic/payflow/integration-gu	Get Payflow integrati
-1 Not found: The	https://developer.paypal.com/webapps/developer/docs/classic/bu	API tools

Figure 26

HotJar

Hotjar is online usability tool for testers to analyse where users are going on your website or mobile site visitors by generating heatmaps by action type of click, move and scroll. Also readings can be made to see what users are going with their mouse. See figure 27.

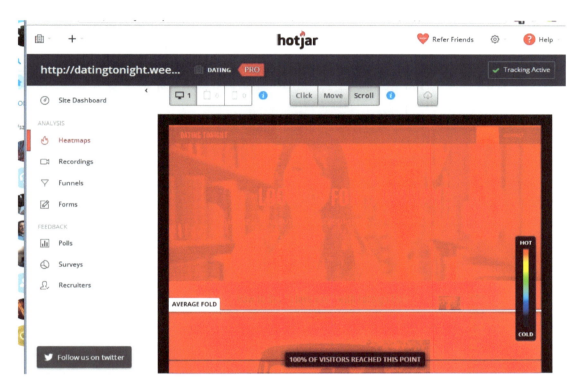

Figure 27

This tool allows you to check the spelling of a web page. It currently only supports English and French. Aspell is used in the back-end. See figure 28.

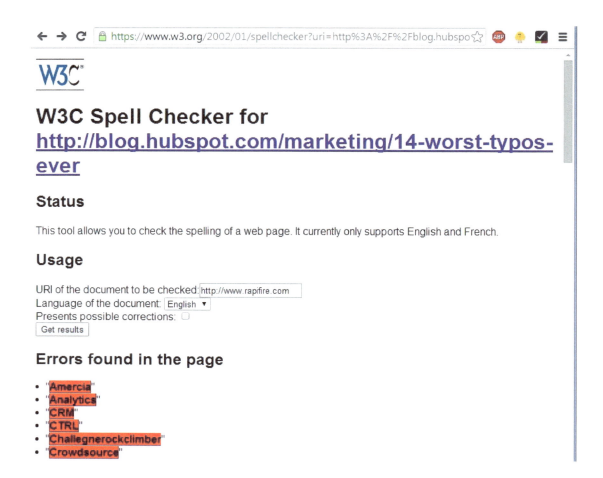

Figure 28

Webpage Spell-Check Chrome Extension

Webpage Spell-check is a Chrome extension that lets you check the spelling directly on the web-page. This way you can easily identify and fix the errors which get missed in your favourite HTML editor even when it has also spell-check support. As this uses the Google Chrome spell checker, so it also shows the corrections for the typo and spelling mistakes and let you edit the typos directly in the web-page. See figure 29.

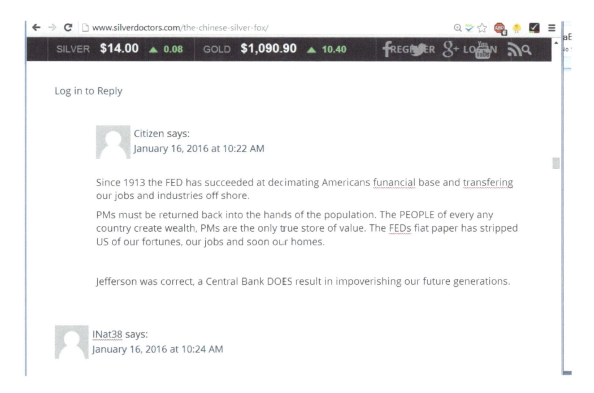

Figure 29

A-Tester

A-Tester is a testing tool for validating compliance of a website with the Web Content Accessibility Guidelines. specifically it checks that the page meets the "WCAG 2.0 Level-AA conformance statements for HTML5 foundation markup" and delivers a report that, in the absence of issues, can act as a very broad and easily confirmed WCAG 2.0 Level-AA claim. Just enter the URL at the top of web page, submit the page and the report appears. See figure 30 and figure 31.

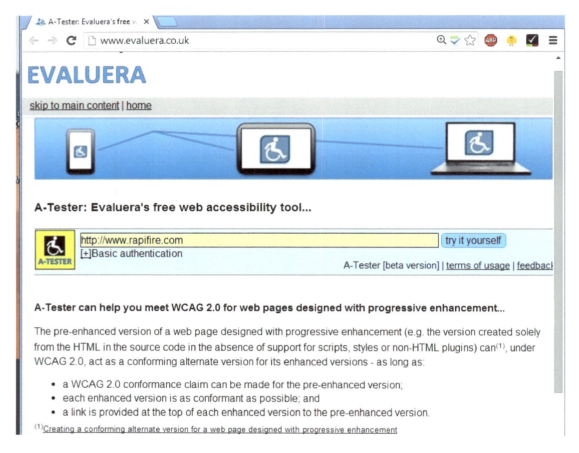

Figure 30

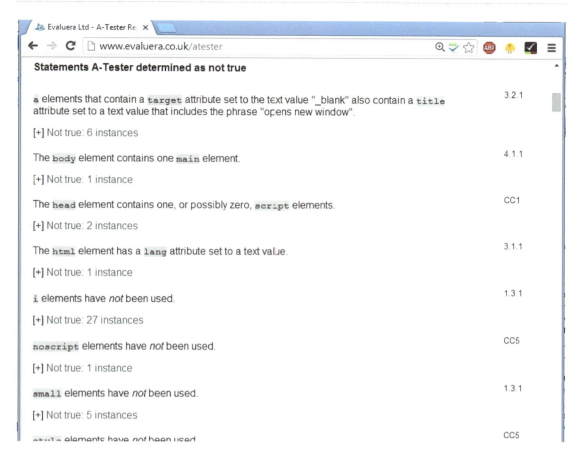

Statements A-Tester determined as not true

`a` elements that contain a `target` attribute set to the text value "_blank" also contain a `title` attribute set to a text value that includes the phrase "opens new window".	3.2.1
[+] Not true: 6 instances	
The `body` element contains one `main` element.	4.1.1
[+] Not true: 1 instance	
The `head` element contains one, or possibly zero, `script` elements.	CC1
[+] Not true: 2 instances	
The `html` element has a `lang` attribute set to a text value.	3.1.1
[+] Not true: 1 instance	
`i` elements have *not* been used.	1.3.1
[+] Not true: 27 instances	
`noscript` elements have *not* been used.	CC5
[+] Not true: 1 instance	
`small` elements have *not* been used.	1.3.1
[+] Not true: 5 instances	
elements have *not* been used	CC5

Figure 31

SEO Centro

Testers don't typically do SEO testing but if nobody does it at your company then you should run some tests to see what can be improved for SEO. The SEO analyser tool by SEO Centro gives testers an in-depth seo analysis of their websites SEO ranking on a page-by-page basis. This tool also shows the website social media ranking, site usability, online reputation, meta tags, and site speed. See figure 33.

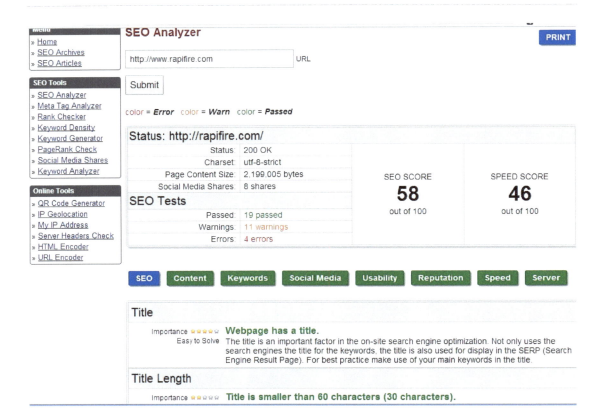

Figure 33

Tenon

Besides having an online tool for testing accessibility on a website URL, Tenon has an API to provide reliable and accurate automated accessibility testing coverage for a wide array of accessibility best practice. WCAG Success Criterion is tested by Tenon and how many tests are provided for each. It is important to understand that no accessibility testing tool can provide complete coverage, even at the single Success Criterion level. See figure 34.

9 issues found for
http://rapifire.com/

⏱ Processed in 2.13sec
Screen Size: 800w x 600h
Page size: 22kb

Download CSV ⬇

Tests = 62

59

11.1%

22.2%

66.7%

Percentage issues per criteria for this page

Error

```
<img src="images/install-client.png" class="ui large i
mage">
```

Test ID 9

Description

🐛 Error / priority 95%
Image missing alt attribute

(line: 141, 11)

Web Content Accessibility Guidelines
(WCAG) 2.0, Level A: 1.1.1 Non-text Content

All images must have an alt attribute. Not
supplying an alt attribute will mean that users
who cannot see the image will not understand
what the image conveys.

Figure 34

Tellurium

Tellurium is an easy-to-use and robust test management and test automation platform. You can create manual tests and English like automated tests for your websites and web apps. Tellurium allows teams to use groups, tags, and playlists to collaborate. See figure 35.

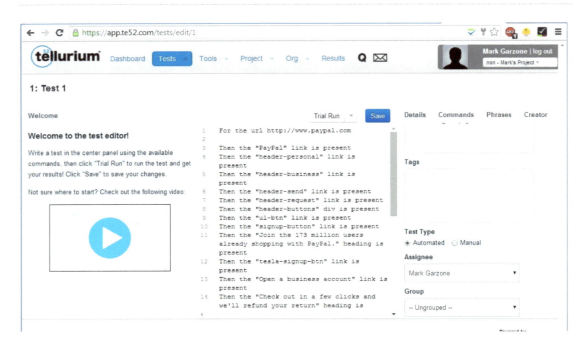

Figure 35

Chapter 3: Security Testing Tools

There are 80 to 90 million plus cybersecurity events per year, with close to 400 new threats every minute, and up to 70 percent of attacks going undetected. You need to run security tests on your app to defend against these threats. Below is a list of such security testing tools which will help you find weaknesses which need to repaired..

SiteDigger

SiteDigger 3.0 is an automated tool for Google Hacking. What is Google Hacking? Google hacking is a computer hacking technique that uses Google Search to find security holes in a website's configuration and computer code. SiteDigger searches Google's cache to look for vulnerabilities, error messages, configuration mistakes, privacy issues, and interesting security nuggets on web sites. Google caches as many web pages as possible during its crawl of the internet. The advantage of searching the Google cache is that the website is not accessed hence website admin does not know that it is being hacked. SiteDigger queries for results that reside in Google's cache by using the *cache:* operator. Including a search term along with the *cache:* operator forces Google to highlight the search term within the cached page. For example, *cache:www.softwaretools.com tools* will show Google's cache of www.softwaretesting.com and highlight the word "tools" on every page it finds.

Google will index many different file formats in addition to the standard HTML file. The *filetype:* operator instructs Google to return only the file types specified in the search string. The query filetype:xls "for internal use only" will return all excel spreadsheets in Google's index that include the words "for internal use".

SiteDigger also helps companies with the prohibition of workers using their work email address to post messages on blogs, and forums. The search strategy *@greatfirm.com* will return all pages where an employee has used their @greatfirm.com email address on the internet. This may also return many results from your company site, but this can be filtered out those results by using the '-' character and the site: operator together. See figure 36 and 37.

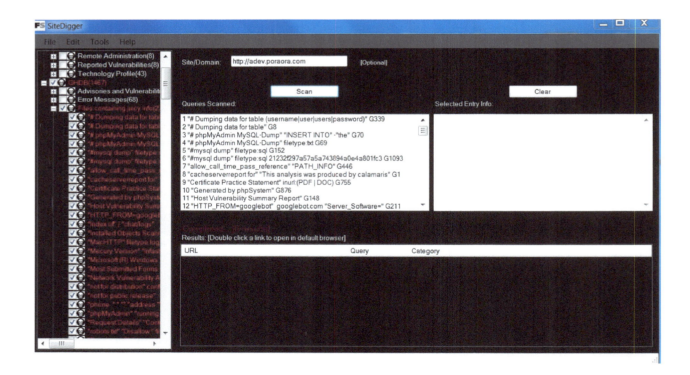

Figure 36

filetype:xls "for internal use only"

All   Images   Videos   News   More ▾   Search tools

About 1,030 results (0.59 seconds)

Internal Use Only - farnell.com
Ad pl.farnell.com/InternalUseOnly ▾
Zamów Internal Use Only W Cenie 10.86zl Wysyłamy Tego Samego Dnia

[XLS] Relocation Form - California State University San Marcos
https://www.csusm.edu/travel/262%20Relocation.xls
2, RELOCATION TRAVEL EXPENSE CLAIM, For Internal Use Only. 3, CSUSM 262 -
Rev. 01/2015, PU, PR, NF SS, CA. 4, CLAIMANT'S NAME, EXT. DEPT.

[XLS] Order Form - Thermo Fisher Scientific
https://tools.thermofisher.com/.../GeneArt_Precision_TALs_Request_For... ▾
Red background color indicates wrong length or missing 'T' at 5') *, Functional Vector *, Data
for internal use only, Glycerol stock of E. coli, Optional only for TAL ...

[XLS] Project Information Sheet - Catalog - CULTEC, Inc.

Figure 37

Vega Scanner

Vega is a java based open source web security scanner and testing
platform. The scanner scans vulnerabilities for SQL Injection, Cross-
Site Scripting (XSS), and inadvertently disclosed sensitive information.

Vega can be extended using a JavaScript API. Also included is an intercepting proxy to monitor the traffic. See figure 38.

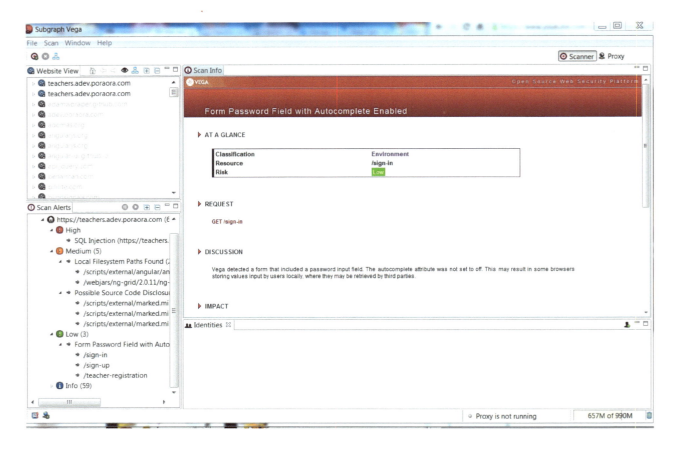

Figure 38

OllyDbg

Windows based debugger used for analysing buffer overflow vulnerabilities. It can be used for binary code when source is unavailable to plan penetration attacks. See figure 39.

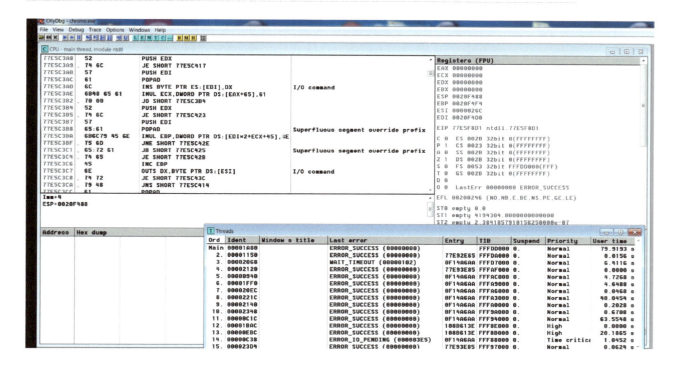

Figure 39

SearchDiggity

SearchDiggity 3.1 is the primary attack tool of the Google Hacking Diggity Project. It is Bishop Fox's MS Windows GUI application that serves as a front-end to the most recent versions of our Diggity tools: GoogleDiggity, BingDiggity, Bing LinkFromDomainDiggity, CodeSearchDiggity, DLPDiggity, FlashDiggity, MalwareDiggity, PortScanDiggity, SHODANDiggity, BingBinaryMalwareSearch, and NotInMyBackYard Diggity. See figure 40.

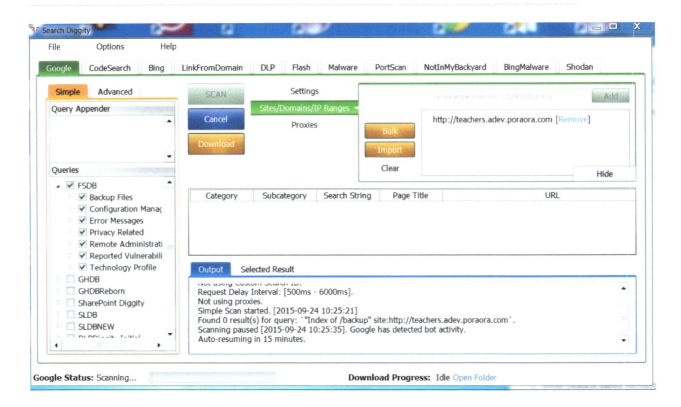

Figure 40

Symantec CryptoReport and Wormly

Legacy and new web servers are often able and configured to handle weak cryptographic options.

Even if high grade ciphers are normally used and installed, some server misconfiguration could be used to force the use of a weaker cipher to gain access to the supposed secure communication channel. There several online tools which run such tests such as Symantec Cryptoreport and wormly to check for cipher weaknesses. See figure 41 and 42.

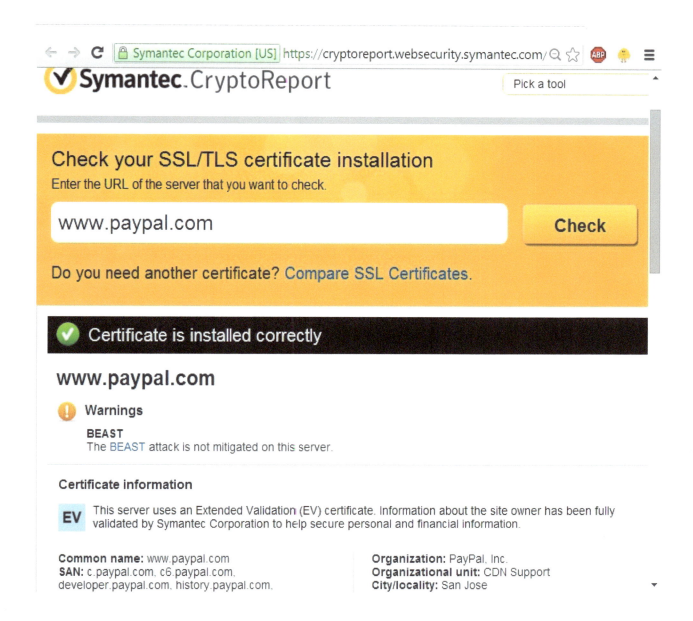

Figure 41

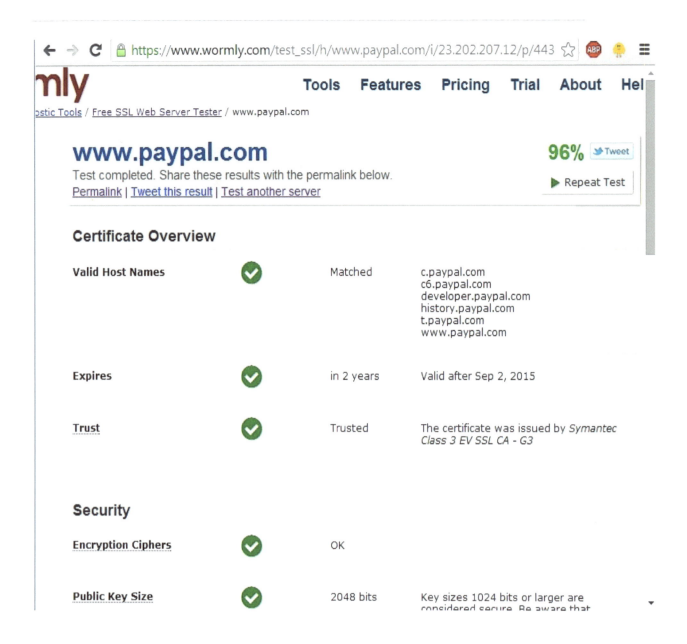

Figure 42

Wireshark

Wireshark is a free and open-source packet analyzer. It is used for network troubleshooting, analysis, software and communications protocol development, and education. Wireshark is software that "understands" the structure (encapsulation) of different networking protocols. It can parse and display the fields, along with their meanings as specified by different networking protocols. The user typically sees packets highlighted in green, blue, and black. Wireshark lets the user put network interface controllers that support promiscuous mode into that mode, so they can see all traffic visible on that interface, not just traffic addressed to one of the interface's configured addresses and broadcast/multicast traffic. You can set filter rules to narrow the traffic on the source and destination address and port. Wireshark uses colors to help the user identify the types of traffic at a glance. By default, green is TCP traffic, dark blue is DNS traffic, light blue is UDP traffic, and black identifies TCP packets with problems such as delivered out-of-order. See figure 43 and 44.

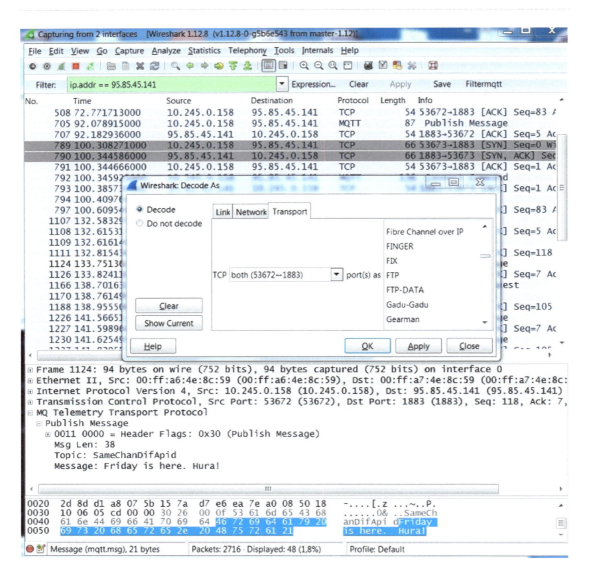

Figure 43

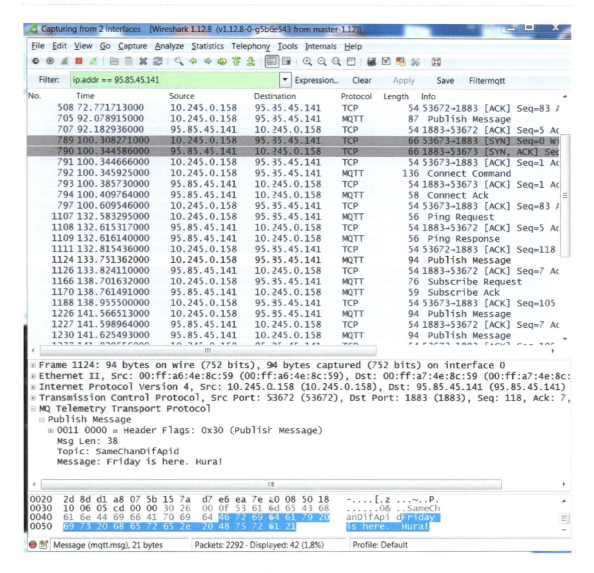

Figure 44

Unmask Parasites

This online website tool Unmask Parasites is a security service that assists you in revealing hidden embedded content inserted by hackers into your web page using various security holes. It is useful for running on your website after it has been put into production for a while.

This technique of embedding hidden content is used mostly by spammers who insert hundreds of hidden links to web sites advertising medications, cheap loans and adult oriented websites.

Another example of hidden malicious content is code that redirects visitors who click on your site's search results in Google to completely different web sites owned by spammers. This sort of exploit is hard to detect by site owners, since the malicious code redirects only for first time visitors.

What all these techniques have in common is that they parasitize benign web sites in order to take advantage of their search engine ranking, visitors which is paid for by their victims. See figure 45.

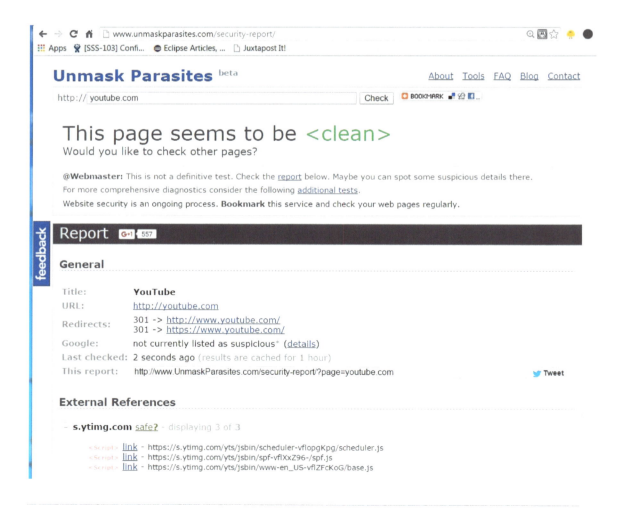

Figure 45

Chapter 4: Mobile Testing Tools

The number of active mobile devices and human beings crossed over somewhere around the 7.19 billion mark in 2014. Testing mobile apps is very important since they are everywhere. This chapter covers mobile testing tools for testing functionality and system performance.

Eggplant

eggPlant is a software image recognition testing tool for conducting mobile testing using the iOS and Android Gateway agents such as VNC server to connect directly to real mobile devices or emulators. This allows it to fully test mobile apps on iOS, Android, Windows Phone, BlackBerry, and other mobile devices. The benefits of image based testing are the following:

- One script for all devices and all platforms.

- No jail-breaking.

- Full device control.

- No modification of the app.

eggPlant's scripting language is SenseTalk. When the script is executed, eggPlant finds the image wherever it is on screen using image recognition algorithms and performs the scripted action. So the test runs even if the UI objects and outputs are in different locations on the screen, for any reason. If an image cannot be found, SenseTalk's ImageFound() function returns FALSE, so the script can raise an incident. See figure 46 and figure 47.

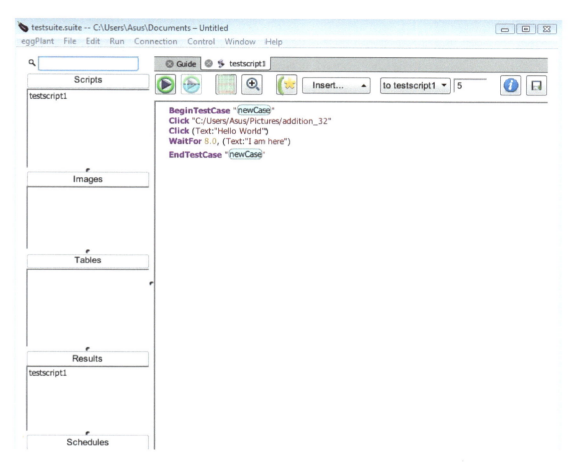

Figure 46

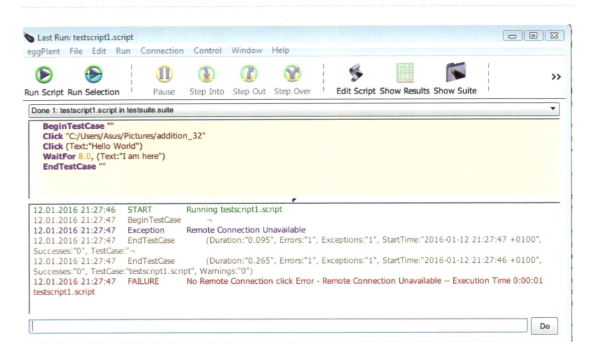

Figure 47

adb.exe Tool for Getting Android Logs

The logs for an android device are stored in circular memory buffers in the device. You can view these logs to check for exceptions or other application logs using the adb.exe tool found in the platform-tools directory of your android SDK. To do so, first check the USB debugging checkbox in your System Settings -> Developer Settings. See figure 48.

Figure 48

Then connect your phone to your computer using a USB cable. Next run the cmd command "adb devices" to get the list of devices connected. Typically you will see only 1 device if you are not using an emulator at the time when connected to the phone.

C:\Users\Asus\android-sdks\platform-tools>adb devices

List of devices attached

0123456789ABCDEF   device

C:\Users\Asus\android-sdks\platform-tools>

If you want to save the whole logs to a file without filtering use the command "adb logcat > logs.txt". See figure 49.

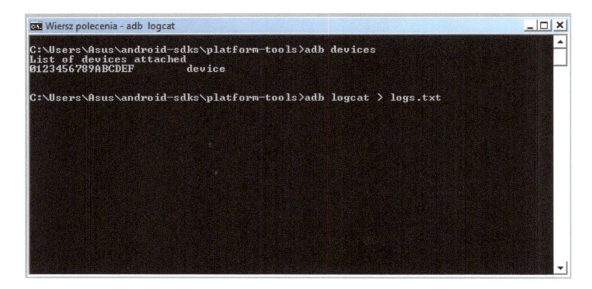

Figure 49

Next run on Windows the command "adb logcat | findstr Exception" to filter the output to show only exceptions. Use "adb logcat | grep Exception" for Linux. See figure 50.

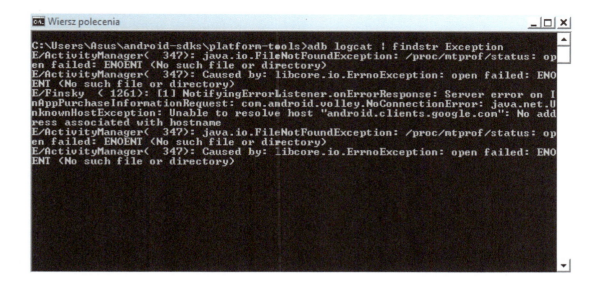

Figure 51

Alternatively you can install a logcat viewer from Google Play such as Catlog and run it to see the logcat entries. See figure 52.

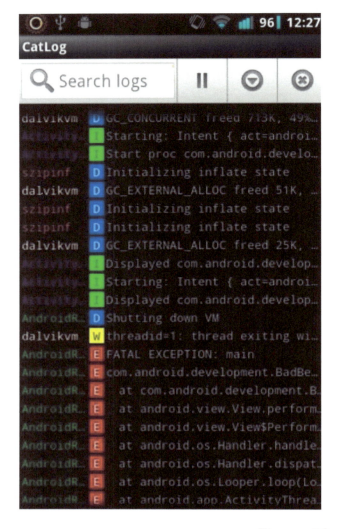

Figure 52

CPU Monitor Advanced Lite

For CPU monitoring and battery usage there are many tools in Google Play. A good tool to install CPU Monitor is CPU Monitor Advanced Lite is an expert technical app which records historical information about processes running on your device. The app also permits you to graph the CPU, the memory and the battery drain. See figures 53, 54, 55, and 56

Figure 53

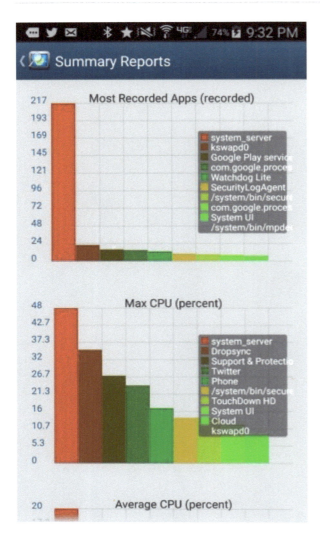

Figure 54

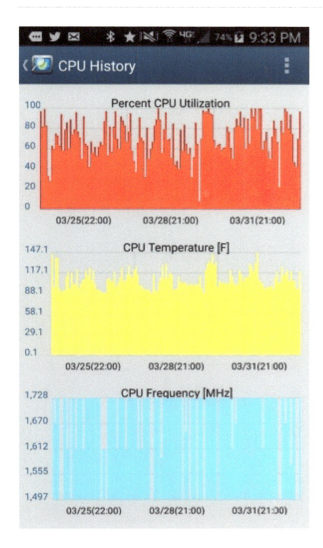

Figure 55

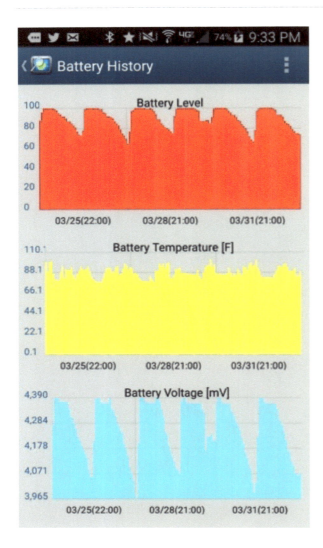

Figure 56

TestObject

TestObject is a mobile testing platform with hundreds of real devices, accessible directly from any browser. Testers can upload their apps onto devices and see if and how they perform. Along with the devices, the company offers automated testing by running scripts for Robotium, Espresso and Appium tests. See figures 57 and 58.

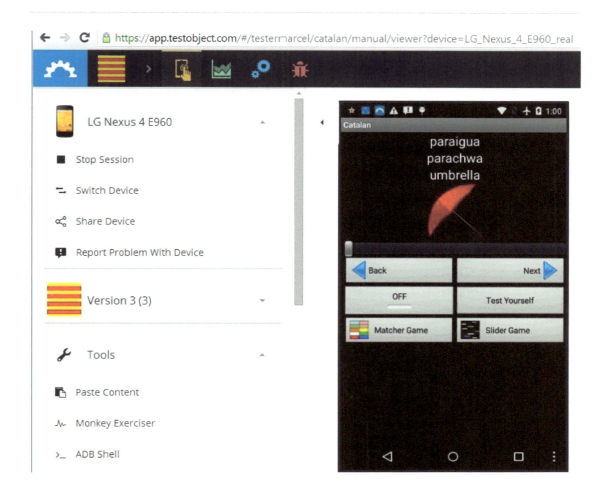

Figure 57

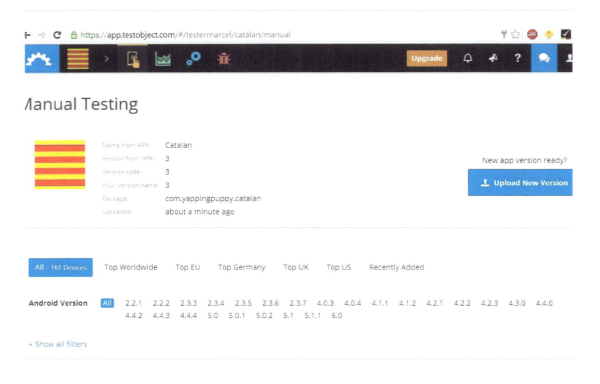

Figure 58

Scan

Scan is an easy-to-use open source free command line tool that runs tests of your iOS and Mac app. It works perfectly with fastlane and other tools. It uses a plain xcodebuild command, therefore keeping 100% compatible with xcodebuild.

Here is an example of running scan.

```
scan --workspace "Example.xcworkspace" --scheme "AppName" --device "iPhone 6" –clean
```

Scan uses xcpretty to produce a good looking output. You can always access the raw output in ~/Library/Logs/scan. See figure 59.

Figure 59

ZAPTEST

ZAPTEST is a software test automation solution for testing applications Cross-Platform. ZAPTEST allows testing of any GUI based software on any modern OS, mobile or conventional including iOS, Android, WinMo, Blackberry, Windows, Mac, and Linux, and supports testing of Agile and CI (DevOps) development. The community version is free which allows you to test web, new windows apps or mobile apps. See figures 60, 61 and 62.

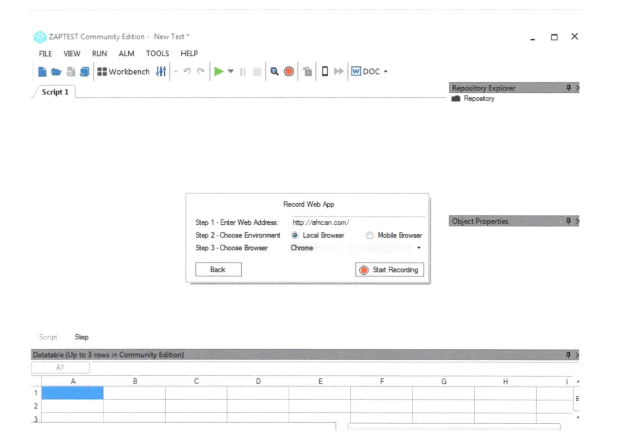

Figure 60

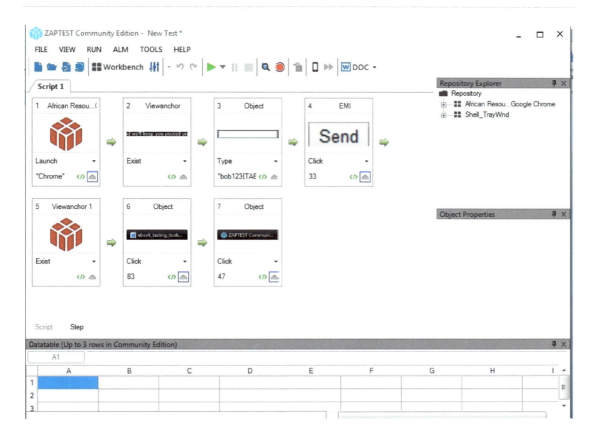

Figure 61

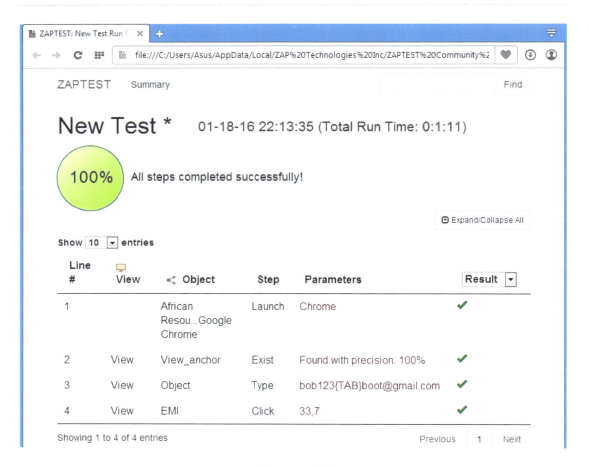

Figure 62

Chapter 5: Performance Testing Tools

What is performance driven development? It is an extension of test driven development in which performance goals of the software must be met. This is achieved with performance testing tools for load testing and page loading speed.

GTmetrix

If you notice that your website page loads slowly you can report a bug ticket about this with a linkin the bug description to the GTmetrix website. This website tool analyses what is wrong with the website and gives tips on how to fix it for developers who need to optimize the websites loading performance. The tool analyses according to Google Pagespeed and Yslow gives grade rating. A free handy feature is that it can monitor you website and send an email alert when the loading performance fails below a set criteria. Other features are below. See figures 63 and 64.

- Gathering key performance indicators such as Page Load Time, Total Page Size and Total # of Requests.

- Analysing your page on a rea Android device.

- Testing your page from multiple regions around the world.

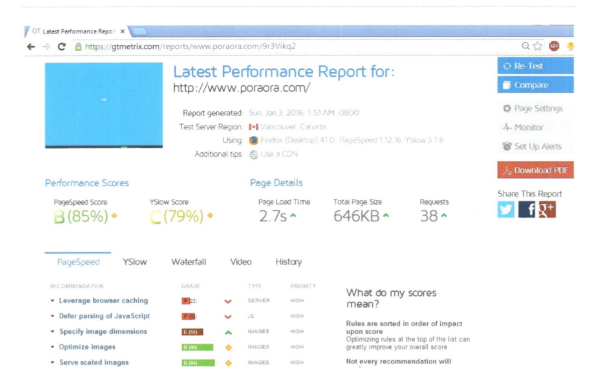

Figure 63

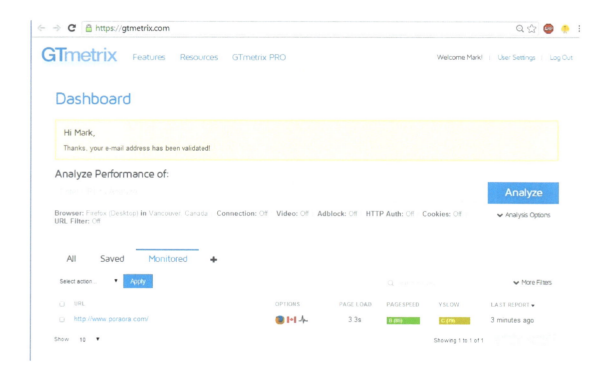

Figure 64

LoadWise

LoadWise is a simple performance load testing tool with a script recorder for Firefox. It can be used also for functional tests. It comes with 3 maximum users for free and the paid version overcomes this limitation. See figures 65 and 66

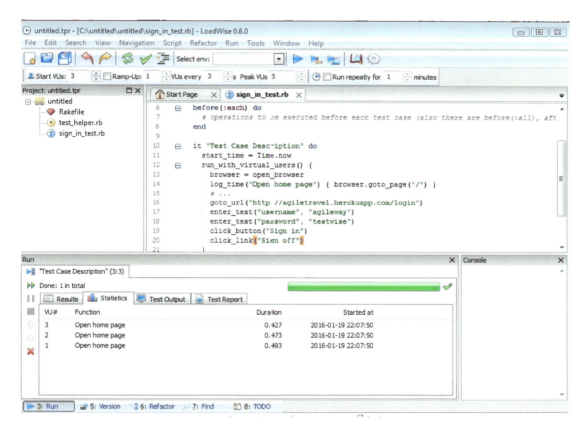

Figure 65

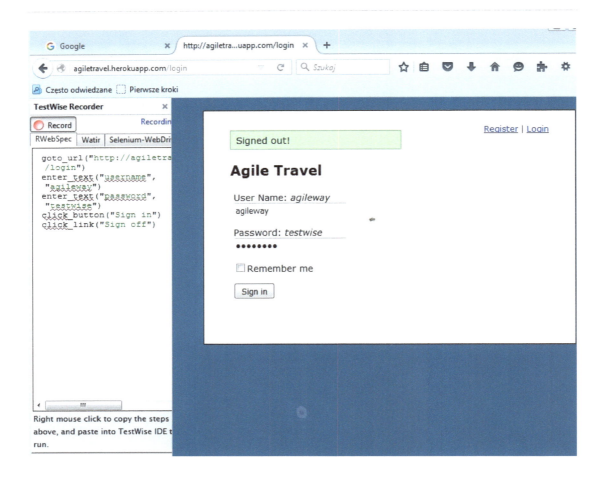

Figure 66

Badboy

Badboy is a powerful open source tool designed for automation testing and load testing complex web applications. Badboy makes web testing and development easier with dozens of features including a simple yet comprehensive capture/replay interface, powerful load testing support, detailed reports, and graphs. It is similar to JMeter in many respects but handles AJAX requests better. See figure 67.

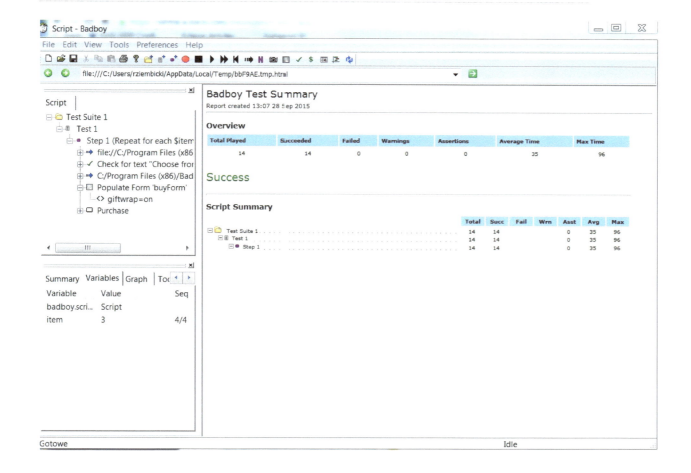

Figure 67

Webperformance

Webperformance is a commercial load testing tool without needing to install apps and configuring server. The starter test tool can create tests based on a URL and recorder. And if you want help, their experts are a click away. See figure 68 and figure 69.

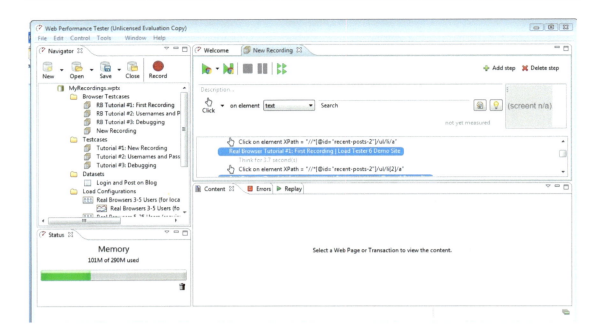

Figure 68

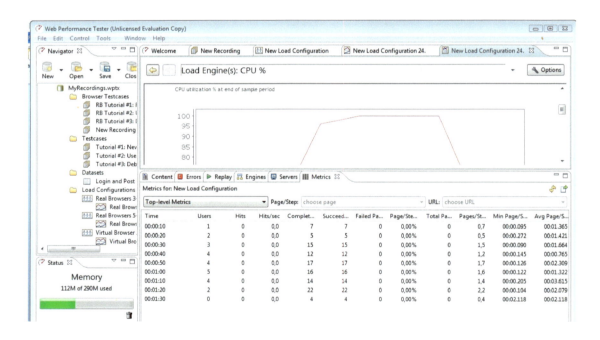

Figure 69

WebPagetest

WebPagetest is an open source tool used for measuring and analyzing the performance of web pages. After submitting the URL it generartes a report for page level metrics which includes load time, fully loaded time, first byte time, start render time, speed index, DOM elements, and a return code. See figure 70.

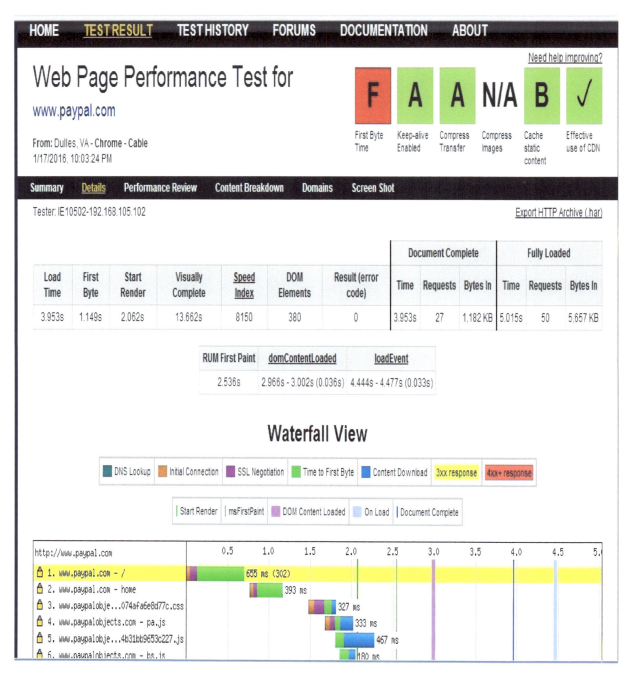

Figure 30

Loader.io

Loader.io is a free load testing service that allows you to stress test your webapps and APIs with 1000s of concurrent connections. All that you need to do is upload a token file to verify your website and then run a test. Tests can be scheduled to run at a later time. See figure 31.

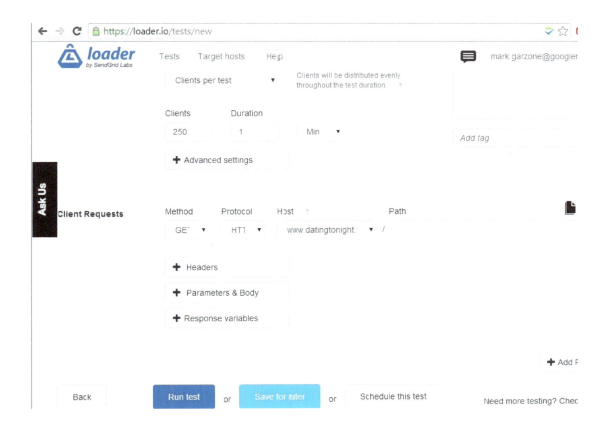

Figure 32

SourceMonitor

The freeware program SourceMon tor lets you see inside your software source code to find out how much code you have and to identify the relative complexity of your modules. SourceMonitor provides the following below. See figures 70 and 71. Below are some of it's features.

- Collects metrics in a fast, single pass through source files at speeds of 10,000 lines of code per second.

- Measures metrics for source code written in C++, C, C#, VB.NET, Java, Delphi, Visual Basic (VB6) or HTML.

- Saves metrics in checkpoints for comparison during software development projects.

- Displays and prints metrics in tables and charts, including Kiviat diagrams.

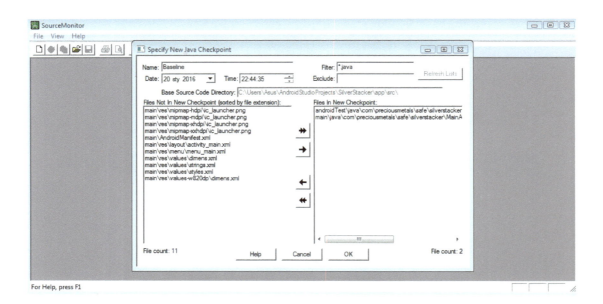

Figure 70

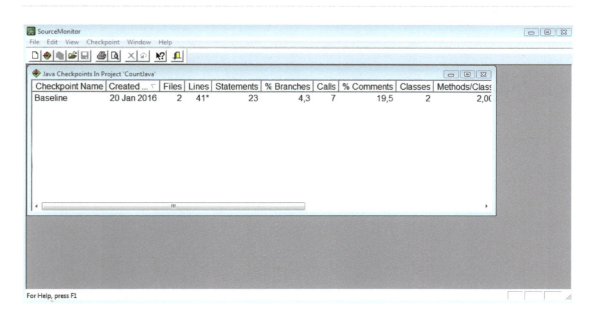

Figure 71

Conclusion

There are many testing tools on the market which can help you with your testing. Select free open source tools over paid tools as open source tools can be customized if needed to add missing functionality, and often have less bugs in them. Before rolling out the testing tool to the whole company, the tool should be tested for a trial period to prove the tool's effectiveness. Often it's a good idea to evaluate several tools at once to see which tool is better and meets your testing needs. That's it. Now go head and experiment with new tools. Happy testing!

Alphabetical Index